ROMAN LONDON'S AMPHITHEATRE

NICK BATEMAN

First published in November 2000 as *Gladiators at the Guildhall*
Revised edn 2011
© Museum of London 2011

A CIP catalogue record for this book is available from the British Library

ISBN 978-1-901992-87-8

**Written, designed and photographed by
Museum of London Archaeology**

Illustrations: Faith Vardy (finds drawings and reconstructions),
Carlos Lemos, Peter Hart-Allison and Hannah Faux (plans),
Mark Burch and Sarah Jones (geomatics) and Judith Dobie
(reconstruction paintings)
Photography and reprographics: Andy Chopping, Maggie Cox
and Ed Baker
Editor: Sue Hirst
Design and production: Tracy Wellman

Cover: gladiators in combat on a sherd of imported samian pottery
found in London

CONTENTS

ACKNOWLEDGEMENTS

Museum of London Archaeology (MOLA) gratefully acknowledges the help of the City of London Corporation, who generously sponsored all of the Guildhall site fieldwork and the subsequent analysis and publication of the findings. Particular thanks are due to Ted Hartill, the City Surveyor, who oversaw the development of the Guildhall Art Gallery site – and the archaeological work that preceded it – on behalf of the Guildhall Yard East Building Committee, together with Ray Hatchard of the City Surveyors' Department and Michael Bankover, the City's liaison officer for the project. Gill Andrews acted as the City's archaeological consultant during the analysis and publication stages of the project and provided invaluable advice and support.

MOLA's work on the site was aided by many people and organisations, too numerous to name here, but special thanks are extended to John Wells and Jim Crooks of W S Atkins, and Mike West of Oscar Faber, for all their patience and help over several years of fieldwork. We would also like to thank Ellen Barnes of English Heritage, who as the Inspector of Ancient Monuments for London played a vital role in the implementation of the archaeological programme from its outset.

Within the archaeological team acknowledgement is particularly due to Gina Porter, who co-directed parts of the excavation from 1992 onwards. Thanks also go to Ian Blair (site supervision), Jackie Keily (finds) and Angus Stephenson (site project management), all of whom were involved in the fieldwork project for many years. Without the hard work and dedication of the field team, made up of over 60 Museum of London staff, the completion of the project would not have been possible.

A panoramic view over Londinium in *c* AD 200 with the Thames in the background; the amphitheatre is in the lower centre, close to the rectangular fort

A large team of specialist staff was involved in the post-excavation assessment of the site findings and their work made it possible to produce a popular book about the discoveries in 2000, only a year after the completion of the last excavation. Since that date the team has been involved in careful analysis of the site findings, leading to the publication of two academic monographs in 2007 and 2008, covering the medieval and Roman sequences respectively.

This revision of the popular book has benefited from the analysis work, allowing a comprehensive update concentrating on the Roman findings alone. Grateful acknowledgement goes to Carrie Cowan and Robin Wroe-Brown (co-authors of the Roman monograph), Richard Macphail (micromorphology), Ian Betts (building materials), Beth Richardson (pottery), Joanna Bird (samian), Angela Wardle (small finds), John Shepherd (glass), Damian Goodburn (timber), Ian Tyers (tree-ring dating) and the many other contributors. The initial revision and updating of the text was carried out by Peter Rowsome.

Kieron Heard and Nick Bateman recording the amphitheatre arena wall, found on the site of the new Guildhall Art Gallery

View of the amphitheatre display beneath the Guildhall Art Gallery, looking west towards the arena

BEGINNINGS

A DAY OF DISCOVERY

It was cold, wet and very muddy in the deep hole near the City of London's Guildhall in February 1988, and the archaeological team was nearing the end of five months' excavation. Things had gone more or less according to plan. The foundations of a medieval chapel had been recorded, some 17th-century burials had been found, and there were even some unexpected Roman remains – walls at unusual angles – at the bottom of the six small trenches being dug. All in all, it had been a routine excavation for that area; the archaeologists were already thinking about the next site they would be going on to.

One day it rained even more than usual – layers of soil turned to mud, colour distinctions became unclear and the paper forms used for keeping records disintegrated. On days like this it was best to stay in the small hut used as a site office, turn up the fire, and work on the backlog of written and drawn records.

As the excavation supervisor, I was curious about the strange Roman walls: 'Why don't you draw them all on one plan', I said to one of the team, 'and check out their levels at the same time …'. Later that day we looked at the plan. The alignment of the walls still looked very odd. But the strangest thing was that they all lay at precisely the same depth in the ground. Further checking revealed that they were all built in the same way – 1.2m (4ft) thick, with two courses of red tile at the bottom and rough stonework above. Surely this couldn't just be a coincidence? Yet how could the odd angles fit together? The Romans constructed buildings with right angles.

I gathered the whole team, 12 of us, around the table and asked for ideas. The site archive does not record who first suggested 'What if *that* wall was curved?' but things moved fast from there. 'How many Roman buildings are there with curved walls?' … 'It's too big for a temple' … 'A theatre, perhaps?' … 'No, it's an amphitheatre!'

Within a day some of the country's leading Roman historians and archaeologists were on site, excitement mounting. Everyone agreed – we had found Londinium's amphitheatre.

Paul Travis cleaning Roman timbers at the Guildhall site after heavy rainfall

NO GREAT EXPECTATIONS …

Guildhall Art Gallery was created in 1886, in buildings on the east side of Guildhall Yard which had previously been used as courts of law. The buildings were badly damaged in German bombing during 1940. After they were finally demolished in 1987, to make way for a new art gallery, Museum of London archaeologists were called in to conduct a 'routine' excavation before construction work started. No one was expecting anything spectacular, although remains of the medieval Guildhall chapel were known to survive. But in 1988 the Roman amphitheatre was discovered. Following a hiatus in work, during which the new building was redesigned, excavation restarted in 1992 and continued, on and off, until shortly before the new Guildhall Art Gallery was opened by the Queen in November 1999. Specialist analysis of all the archaeological finds and records was completed in 2008 and published in two academic monographs.

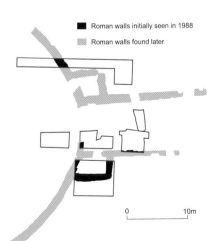

■ Roman walls initially seen in 1988

▨ Roman walls found later

Very little of the amphitheatre was visible in the narrow trenches excavated during 1987–8, making interpretation of the walls difficult

0   10m

7

A UNIQUE OPPORTUNITY

The discovery of the Guildhall amphitheatre in 1988 was proclaimed on national and international television and radio. The *Observer* of 28 February described it as 'one of the most exciting archaeological finds since the Second World War'. The *Sunday Telegraph* (6 March) called it 'one of the most important [finds] in Britain this century'.

Amphitheatres are, almost by definition, exciting buildings. Very few have been excavated in Britain, and London's amphitheatre had been sought, unsuccessfully, for 100 years. London's amphitheatre site is important not just for its Roman evidence, as the ruins were used as the basis for a small Late Saxon trading settlement, with closely-packed wooden houses, animal pens

The discovery of London's amphitheatre made national headlines in February 1988

An artist's view of the site during excavations in 1988; the high brick walls which dominate the scene are the remains of Victorian basements, with the amphitheatre walls – shown here in pastel colours – lying at much deeper levels and reached only after weeks of careful digging

and alleys representing some of the best-preserved 11th-century remains in Europe. In the 13th century the site witnessed the construction of London's Guildhall, which, along with associated buildings such as the Guildhall chapel, developed into the political and economic heart of the medieval City of London.

At every age, the Guildhall site has been at the centre of the dynamic interplay between private and public in the City of London. The monuments which emerged – Roman amphitheatre, medieval Guildhall – were a product of that dynamic tension, with trade creating wealth and the wealth demanding display.

There is not enough space in this book to mention all of the important archaeological discoveries from the site, even for the Roman period alone, and a full description of the findings is contained within the two academic monographs about the site. They are listed in the *Further reading* section at the back of this book. This book attempts to cover the most exciting finds and also to present the big picture relating to what essentially is a fascinating, and human, story of the development of Roman Londinium.

Filming of the archaeological work at the east end of the amphitheatre in 1993; in the foreground a metal detector is used to search through excavated soil for some of the thousands of metal artefacts recovered from the site

A series of plastic-covered canopies spanned the site of the 1992–3 dig to protect the delicate remains from the weather

PUBLIC MUNIFICENCE

At the peak of its development in the 15th century, the Guildhall complex, with its courts, fountains, tall buildings and imposing entrances, might be described as the very model of medieval public munificence. Strangely, however, the very word 'munificence' carries distant echoes of the Guildhall's own peculiar past. The word is derived from the Latin *munus*, a gift or duty. But *munus* had another meaning as well; it was the word used by the Romans for a gladiatorial display – a show originally put on as a 'duty' by a member of the upper classes seeking preferment.

ARCHAEOLOGY IN LONDON

Today's London is getting bigger as the population increases and there is growing pressure for development on both greenfield (undeveloped) and brownfield (former industrial) lands. A hundred years ago places like Bexley, Chingford and Acton were a part of the countryside. This expansion has taken place, on and off, for nearly 2000 years. Archaeological evidence for London's growing suburbs has been found at many sites. At the same time the City, the heart of historic London, was the subject of repeated rebuilding, with the result that the modern street level there is up to 6m (almost 20ft) above the ground surface upon which the Romans founded Londinium. This remarkable rise in ground level is the result of the individual actions of Londoners, who have been pulling down or burning down old buildings, renovating or building their homes, burying their refuse, and generally landscaping and levelling the ground repeatedly. The City of London is, quite literally, built on rubbish. Identifying and peeling back those layers is the business of archaeology.

Recorded archaeological investigation in London may have started with the workmen who uncovered a Roman kiln during Sir Christopher Wren's rebuilding of St Paul's after the Great Fire of 1666. In the 19th century a new hobby, 'antiquarian observation', became popular amongst the middle classes. In the great Victorian rebuilding of London many chance observations were made – Roman mosaics, Saxon pots, medieval burials – and reports on finds were sent to journals like the *Gentleman's Magazine*. The bombing of the City of London in World War II caused extensive destruction, leading to a rash of redevelopment projects in the 1950s and 60s, and prompting a similar leap in archaeological work as rescue excavations were mounted by Professor Grimes with teams of volunteers.

Antiquarian painting of Roman and medieval artefacts from the City of London

ARCHAEOLOGICAL WORK BY **MOLA**

Museum of London Archaeology (MOLA) provides archaeological services in London, the UK and abroad. Projects are normally funded by the developer or landowner and can range from small excavations lasting a few days to major projects that can last for months to years. The results of fieldwork, where significant archaeological evidence is discovered, is the subject of careful analysis. The results may be published in short technical reports, journal articles or – in the case of the largest and most important investigations such as that at Guildhall Yard – as books containing both academic and popular accounts of the findings.

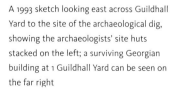

A 1993 sketch looking east across Guildhall Yard to the site of the archaeological dig, showing the archaeologists' site huts stacked on the left; a surviving Georgian building at 1 Guildhall Yard can be seen on the far right

A lot of archaeological remains were destroyed without record during this period and it was quickly realised that the pace of redevelopment required greater resources. As a result, the Museum of London's first professional archaeological unit, the Department of Urban Archaeology, was born in 1973. In 1991 the DUA merged with other London archaeological units to become the Museum of London Archaeology Service (MoLAS), now MOLA. The Guildhall site was its first major excavation.

A LATE [RED]START

There was a hiatus in activity on the Guildhall Art Gallery site following the 1988 discovery of the amphitheatre, whilst new plans for the integration of archaeological work and construction were finalised. During this time much of the site 'returned to nature' and recommencement of excavations

in 1992 had to be delayed for several weeks when a black redstart (a protected species) was found to have built its nest in bushes that had grown on this temporary urban wasteland.

Archaeologists excavating and recording Roman walls and surfaces at the amphitheatre

A BRIEF HISTORY OF ROMAN LONDON

Britain finally entered the annals of recorded history with Julius Caesar's two 'invasions' of 55 and 54 BC. Although the Romans thought of them as barbarians, the Britons were, especially in the south-east, already heavily influenced by Roman culture. In the century following these failed attempts to conquer Britain there was a continued and growing trade with the Continent, as well as political links following Caesar's treaties with the principal British tribal leaders. Rome certainly had friends among the Britons.

In AD 43 Emperor Claudius ordered a new invasion and attempt at the complete subjugation of Britain. This invasion was more thorough and successful than that of Julius Caesar, with most of the south-east overrun within a year. The Romans, under the personal leadership of Claudius himself, seized the most important British town in the south, Camulodunum (Colchester), turning it into a military base. Campaigning then pushed towards the midlands and the west to subjugate remaining areas of resistance in the lowlands.

Although Britain, or rather what is now England and Wales, was not fully conquered until the early AD 80s, there was clearly considerable confidence amongst the invaders. Some tribes were openly pro-Roman and quickly adopted Roman customs and laws. In other areas Roman settlers, usually retired soldiers, formed colonies (eg at Camulodunum).

At some time in the late AD 40s, two small hills on the north side of the Thames – now occupied by St Paul's cathedral and Leadenhall market – were selected as the site for a new town. This settlement, called Londinium, may have been run by traders who handled the importing of luxury goods (wine, oil, cloth) to the new province, while exporting raw materials such as minerals and slaves. The new town occupied a strategic site – the lowest bridgeable point on the Thames – and benefited from easy access to the sea and a position at the borders rather than the centres of existing tribal groups. It became the hub of the road network and grew quickly. By the early 2nd century AD, the Roman historian Tacitus was able to describe Londinium as 'famous for its wealth of traders and commercial traffic'.

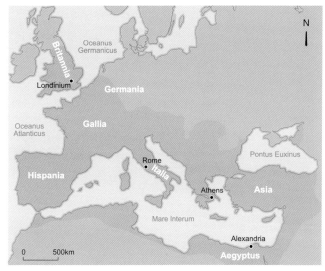

The north-western part of the Roman Empire in the mid 1st century AD

A RAIDING PARTY

The historian Strabo, writing shortly after Caesar's death, said that 'Caesar crossed twice to the island, but came back in haste, without accomplishing much or proceeding very far inland. He won two or three victories over the Britons, even though he took over only two legions, bringing back hostages, slaves and much other booty.' Britain was always seen by the Romans as very remote: writing of the behaviour of the legions in Britain during the civil wars which racked the Roman world in AD 69, Tacitus suggests that 'at such a distance they were divided from the rest of the world by the ocean'.

Emperor Claudius (reigned AD 41–54) led the first invasion of Britain. Claudius was established as emperor after he was found hiding behind a curtain in the palace when his nephew Caligula was murdered. Claudius survived for 13 years in power, suggesting that he was not the fool Roman historians made him out to be

MISERABLE, MISTY AND MARGINAL?

Many Roman writers saw Britain as miserable, misty and marginal. On the other hand, Eumenius (secretary to Emperor Constantius Chlorus who died in York) described Britain in the 3rd century AD as a land that 'the state could ill afford to lose, so plentiful are its harvests, so numerous the pasturelands in which it rejoices'. Which of these views is correct?

Study of the remains of plants, animals and soils from excavations has led us to believe that the widespread clearance of prehistoric woodlands – for cultivation, grazing and timber – had transformed the landscape in south-east Britain long before the Romans arrived. As a result of a worsening climate in the middle of the 1st millennium BC, there was a period of abandonment of land, but by AD 43 British farmers were once again bringing parts of the London region back into cultivation.

The profiles of the original gravel and brickearth subsoils seen in excavations reveal that Londinium was founded upon two low hills, remnants of ancient floodplain terraces along the Thames. Similar gravel terraces follow the river up- and downstream. Ditches have been found marking Romano-British fields, which were probably reclaimed from the scrubby, open woodland.

The Ermine Street Guard, a Roman re-enactment society (Ermine Street runs from London to Lincoln and York, the origins of the A10)

THE INVASION OF AD 43 – AN EARLY VERSION OF D-DAY?
In AD 43 three Roman legions established a beachhead near Richborough in Kent and then pushed north-west to the Thames, where a battle took place and the river was successfully crossed, probably somewhere near Westminster. The Greek historian Dio, writing over a hundred years later, describes what happened.

'The Britons now fell back on the River Thames, at a point near where it enters the sea, and at high tide forms a pool. They crossed over easily because they knew where to find firm ground and easy passage. But the Romans in trying to follow them were not so successful. However the Germans [Roman auxiliary troops] again swam across, and other troops got over by a bridge a little upstream, after which they attacked the barbarians from several sides at once, and killed many of their number. But in pursuing the remainder incautiously some of the troops got into difficulties in the marshes, and a number were lost.'

The banks of the Thames and its low sandy islands may have looked something like this in the 1st century AD

By the time the Romans arrived, it is likely that only scattered trees and copses remained along much of the river's north bank, though surviving stands of oak, hazel, yew, ash and lime trees would have been maintained and exploited, with fruit and berries collected from the woodland-edge, trees coppiced to provide wattle for walls, fences and baskets, and domestic pigs left to forage in the undergrowth. In contrast, a backdrop of thick forest might still have been visible against the northern horizon, cloaking the clay soils of the higher land.

To the south lay the floodplain of the Thames; in AD 43 it was about a mile wide (1.6km) and a broad, shallow river flowed across it, dividing into several channels around low sandy islands. During the 1st millennium BC, the alder carr woodland on the floodplain became inundated by gradually rising river levels. By the Romano-British period, it had been replaced almost everywhere by freshwater reed and sedge fen, brackish marshland and mudflats. Only the highest of the islands in Southwark, Bermondsey and Westminster remained above the encroaching tides and mudflats.

BRITISH WEATHER

Roman writers complained frequently about Britain: 'the weather tends to rain rather than snow. Mist is very common. So that for whole days at a stretch the sun is seen for three or four hours around midday' (Strabo; died c AD 23). 'A thick mist rises from the marshes, so that the atmosphere in the country is always gloomy' (Herodian; c AD 230s). 'What help to the British is the unremitting harshness, the freezing cold, of their climate?' (Claudian; c AD 390s).

The climate improved throughout the Roman period, and by the 3rd and 4th centuries AD it was sufficiently warm and dry for olives and vines to be cultivated in Britain.

An artist's impression of Londinium in c AD 60, looking south-east with the Thames and Southwark in the background; the amphitheatre has not yet been built

AMPHITHEATRES AND GLADIATORS

From the first recorded examples in the 4th century BC, the 'games' in Rome were religious in purpose and character, initially restricted to theatrical performances and chariot racing. Exhibitions of wild beasts as part of these games only started in the mid 2nd century BC. Chariot racing was held for the most part in Rome's Circus Maximus (the long racetrack depicted in the 1959 film *Ben Hur*), and theatrical performances were given in front of the temple of the deity in whose honour the games were held. The games were free to all citizens – indeed they were virtually compulsory, though citizens were never permitted to participate. By the 2nd century AD the six principal sets of annual religious games still accounted for 59 out of a total of 182 days a year for games in Rome, a total which may seem excessive to us today, though the concept of the 'weekend' had not yet been invented!

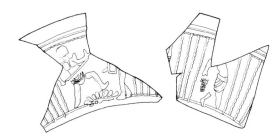

A pair of gladiators (left) with a *retiarius* (right) on sherds of imported samian pottery from the London amphitheatre

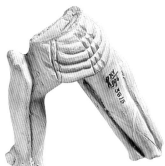

This broken clay figurine of a gladiator, found in London, shows the legs clad in greaves (body armour)

A *retiarius* (net-fighter) in combat against a *secutor* (literally a 'seeker')

The origins of gladiator fighting are shrouded in mystery. Some scholars say that it arose in Campania in southern Italy; others that it developed among the Etruscans, in what is now Tuscany. Most people agree, however, that the tradition of making men fight for the entertainment of others first started in the 4th century BC as a ritual to accompany funerals. This is also what Roman writers themselves believed, such as Livy, writing around the time of the birth of Christ. The first recorded 'public' showing of gladiators in Rome was in 264 BC. It was only at some time in the 1st century BC that gladiator fighting became part of the older 'official' games.

Gladiator fights were staged in many locations: at first, on open ground by the side of funeral pyres; later, surrounded by special temporary stands set up in the town forum. The characteristic elliptical shape of the arena evolved to maximise viewers' lines of sight. Only much later, from the 1st century BC, did the idea of purpose-built and permanent arenas come into existence. The Roman upper classes, the senators, had a real fear that permitting the construction of permanent theatres or amphitheatres, with gatherings of large numbers of citizens, could lead to public expression of political discontent – as indeed it later did.

The word 'gladiator' comes from *gladius*, a sword. There were many types of gladiator, but the main distinctions lay in pairings of lightly and heavily armed men (speed against power; attack against defence; short weapon against long). Traditionally, spectators from the poorest farmer to the Emperor himself were either *scutarii* or *parmularii* – supporters of the 'little shield' or 'big shield' gladiators. Early gladiator types included 'Gauls', 'Samnites' and 'Thracians', all traditional enemies of Rome. During the time of the Emperors there was the popular pairing of *retiarius* (left shoulder armour, net, trident and dagger) against *secutor* (short sword, oval shield, round helmet, greave on left leg). Other types included *murmillones* (heavily armed with crested helmets in the form a fish) and *cataphracti* (with chainmail like Oriental cavalry). In contrast to what is shown in the 2000 film *Gladiator*, there is no evidence that anyone ever fought in the armour of the Roman citizen legionary. Professionals who fought with wild animals were not gladiators but *bestiarii* or *venatores*, and learnt their skills in different training schools.

A trainer overseeing the combat between a *retiarus* (left) and a *secutor* (right); trainers were called *lanistae*, a word believed to be derived from the Etruscan for butcher (image from a mosaic at a villa in Nennig, Germany)

Fragments of glass from London depicting gladiators

The earliest known amphitheatre in the Roman world – the word amphitheatre comes from the Greek, meaning 'theatre on both sides' – is the one at Pompeii, which dates from c 80 BC. The earliest permanent theatre in Rome itself was built in 55 BC, while the earliest stone amphitheatre there was built in 29 BC by a friend of the newly proclaimed emperor, Augustus. The great explosion of arena building across the Empire occurred after the construction of Rome's new amphitheatre (known since the 8th century AD as the Colosseum) in the reign of Emperor Vespasian (AD 69–79).

There was an even greater increase in the popularity of gladiator fighting between c AD 70 and 150. At the celebrations in Rome for Trajan's triumph over the Dacians (in modern-day Romania) at the beginning of the 2nd century AD, 10,000 gladiators fought, and 11,000 wild animals are reported to have been killed. The games lasted 120 days.

View of the eastern entrance and the arena of the stone amphitheatre at Lepcis Magna on the Libyan coast; it held c 16,000 spectators and was built initially in AD 56

EMPEROR VESPASIAN (AD 69–79)
Vespasian was the first emperor not from the family of Augustus and the old aristocracy. He was from respectable provincial stock and had proved himself a capable general fighting in Britain in the AD 40s. A near-contemporary, Tacitus, described him as 'plain-living ... of the old school in his person and table'. Vespasian was responsible for building the Colosseum at Rome and many other large public buildings across the Empire.

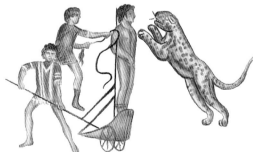

Details from a mosaic at Zliten, Libya, showing executions and *venatores*; one man is bound to a stake on wheels and pushed out to meet his death, another is whipped out to meet his fate; these hapless souls were probably barbarian tribesmen captured in battle; as with other mosaics, it is quite possible that this records a specific show

Gladiator fighting continued until the end of the 4th century AD, when the official gladiator schools in Rome were closed down. The last known fights at Rome took place during the reign of Valentinian III (AD 425–55). Although the new state religion, Christianity, seems to have played a part in the decline of fighting, it does not appear that there was any particular concern for human rights or delicacy about the shedding of blood. Wild beast hunts and the sentencing of criminals to death by wild animals continued into the early 6th century AD. In the western provinces, including Britannia, there is no convincing evidence that any of the arena traditions continued beyond the 3rd century AD.

SPARTACUS

The gladiator Spartacus led an uprising against Rome in 73 BC. Although most of his 70,000 men were runaway slaves, the nucleus of the revolt was formed by a large contingent of gladiators. According to the biographer Plutarch (writing over 100 years later), the revolt started when 78 gladiators escaped from a private barracks and armed themselves by plundering a wagon full of gladiatorial weapons heading for another city. Spartacus and his fellow gladiators were all from outside Italy. They had 'done nothing wrong, but, simply because of the cruelty of their owner, were kept in close confinement' – crammed into living conditions designed for much fewer men. It is remarkable that in the entire 600-year history of gladiator fighting, from the 2nd century BC to the 5th century AD, the only recorded revolt of gladiators occurred about seven years after the first true amphitheatre was built. Whatever the causes of the revolt, it was put down and 6000 survivors were crucified by the side of the road from Rome all the way to Naples.

A still image from Stanley Kubrick's 1960 film *Spartacus*

19

There is no doubt that, even for professionals, being a gladiator was a risky business and most died young. At Verona, Glauco was killed in his eighth fight at the age of 23. The Syrian gladiator Flamma died at 30 after 34 fights, having won 21 times and survived the others. In Rome, Felix died at 45 after receiving Roman citizenship from Emperor Trajan himself. A gravestone at Orange in France commemorates another gladiator who won 53 fights. Winners and survivors frequently ended up as trainers. Gladiators might be one-off volunteers – sometimes even the hot-headed sons of senators fought for the thrill of it – or they might be poor citizens who sold themselves into effective slavery, signing on with the formidable oath 'I undertake to be burnt by fire, to be bound in chains, to be beaten, to die by the sword'. For the great majority, who were not voluntary recruits, being 'condemned to the arena' could be: *ad gladium* – simple unarmed execution in the arena within a year; *ad bestias* – thrown to the wild animals; or *ad ludos* – service as a gladiator with release possible after three years, if you survived.

A small copper-alloy figurine dressed as a Samnite gladiator, wearing a helmet with mask and holding a square shield on the left arm; the right arm may have held a sword or dagger, now missing (from London)

A mosaic from Italy showing gladiators in various stages of combat; the θ (theta) sign indicates the death of the gladiator to the left (th for thanatos, Greek for death); note the gladiators' names

A DAY AT THE AMPHITHEATRE

The spectacles in amphitheatres (the original Latin name for an amphitheatre was a *spectacula*) varied from more or less fair fights, between evenly matched and well-trained gladiators, to simulated hunts in which hundreds of wild animals (many of them specially imported from North Africa) were butchered, to the mass execution and torture of 'criminals' – although the latter might include prisoners of war, slaves and, at certain periods and places, Christians. There was a convention that fighting against animals took place in the morning and proper gladiator fighting in the late afternoon, while executions took place around midday.

TWO FOR THE LIONS

This extract from Lindsey Davis's novel *Two for the lions* (1998) was written about a town in Africa, but it could apply just as well to London. It is some time in June AD 80. We can imagine a new day dawning over London's recently built amphitheatre. The audience is gathering.

The ticket-men were in place, ready to hand out the tokens which assigned places in the various tiers and wedges of seats ... Wineskins

and amphorae had been brought in huge quantities. Snack sellers were hoping for a lucrative day ... Playbills appeared; we got hold of one, but apart from the professional fighters who were listed by names and fighting style, the special bout was only described as a 'combat of three novices'.

After the first arrivals had strolled up, some still eating their breakfasts, the influx suddenly increased and the atmosphere pulsated ... Men wandered about making contacts, perhaps with male business acquaintances, perhaps even with forward women who ought not to have been available.

The rows of seats were filling up fast ... behind us the massed crowds craned their necks from the plain benches that would give them stiff buttocks and backache by the end of the day.

A parade of statues of local gods, crudely disguised under the names of Roman ones, heralded a few brisk religious formalities ... [The governor] was quiet and extremely efficient as he then pronounced the omens good and the procedures all in order. This enabled the games to start.

Gladiatorial shows usually began with a parade of the gladiators, in full array, around the arena; who was to fight with whom was often decided by the drawing of lots, and the fighting was accompanied by martial music; this detail from a mosaic found at Zliten, in North Africa, shows musicians, including a woman playing a water organ, performing in the arena

CONTEMPORARY ATTITUDES

The old republican: the great Roman orator and lawyer Cicero, writing in *c* 50 BC, believed the arena was educational, provided only criminals suffered:

A gladiatorial show is apt to seem cruel and brutal to some eyes, and I incline to think that it is so, as now conducted. But in the days when it was criminals who crossed swords in the death struggle, there could be no better schooling against pain and death, at any rate for the eye.

The man in the street: a surviving Roman novel, a rough and bawdy piece called the Satyricon (1st century AD), provides the perspective of the ordinary man, for whom it was all just bloody entertainment:

And now we are about to have a first class three-day show by gladiators, not a professional troop, but freedmen mostly. Titus will provide the best blades and no quarter, and a slaughterhouse in the middle so the whole amphitheatre can see ... He had already procured as many toughs as you like, a woman to fight from a chariot, and Glyco's steward, who was surprised in bed with his mistress.

The emperor's adviser: with the ironic scorn of the educated classes towards the unrestrained emotions of their inferiors, Seneca (*c* AD 50) discusses a show in which 'criminals' were slaughtered:

I've happened to drop in upon the midday entertainment of the arena in hope of some milder diversions, a spice of comedy, a touch of relief in which men's eyes may find rest after a glut of human blood. No, no: far from it. All the previous fighting was mere softness of heart. Away with such bagatelles: now for the butchery pure and simple! The combatants have nothing to protect them: their bodies are utterly open to every blow: never a thrust but finds its mark. Most people prefer this kind of thing to all other matches ... Naturally so. What good is swordsmanhip? All these things only put off death a little. In the morning men are matched with lions and bears, at noon with their spectators ... 'Kill! Flog! Burn! Why does he jib at cold steel? Why boggle at killing? Why die so squeamishly?'

The Christian: St Augustine, writing in the 4th century AD on the continuing and subversive appeal of the arena, discusses a visit made by a Christian friend. Like Seneca he seems more appalled by the effect on the audience than the sufferings of victims:

The whole place was seething with savage enthusiasm, but he shut the doors of his eyes and forebade his soul to go out into a scene of such evil. If only he could have blocked up his ears too. For in the course of the fight some man fell; there was a great roar from the whole mass of spectators ... he was overcome by curiosity and opened his eyes, feeling perfectly prepared to treat whatever he might see with scorn and to rise above it ... He saw the blood and he gulped down the savagery ... drunk with the lust of blood. He was no longer the man who had come there but was one of the crowd to which he had come.

A re-enactment of gladiatorial combat, staged in front of the City of London's Guildhall as part of a Museum of London exhibition – gladiators are still able to draw a crowd, just as they did 2000 years ago

Artist's depiction of the end of a fight in London's arena, as a British slave appeals for mercy while his triumphant adversary savours victory

GODS, GODDESSES, PRAYERS AND CURSES

The lethal nature of the activities within the arena meant that requests for divine assistance are likely to have been common. A lead figurine found at the London amphitheatre, perhaps of the goddess Juno, is certainly a votive offering, deliberately buried near the eastern entranceway, perhaps to invoke protection for those entering the arena.

Something slightly more sinister is represented by some highly significant finds in the arena – three small inscribed lead 'curse tablets'. Holes in the corners of these suggest they were originally attached to walls, probably inside the amphitheatre. One of them had a complete curse text: 'I give to the goddess Deana [my] headgear and band less one-third. If anyone has done this, whether boy or girl, whether slave or free, I give him, and through me let him be unable to live.'

The wording follows a standard formulaic pattern. The theft of a scarf and hat – perhaps even from someone in the amphitheatre audience – is implicit. The exclusion clause 'whether boy or girl, whether slave or free' is often used in curses aimed at unknown thieves, and a deity's interest was often sought by the gift of a fraction of the stolen property.

A small figurine, probably the goddess Juno, had been deliberately placed near the stone threshold of the amphitheatre's side chamber for beasts

The lead 'curse' to Diana, found in a drain near the arena

Figures from part of a mosaic recording a show given in North Africa (Smirat); the show was presented by a man called Magerius, who commissioned the mosaic for his villa as testimony to his own generosity – a herald in the centre displays a tray with the bags of money spent; the show was a simulated hunt, a *venatio*, in which expensive leopards were pitted against a band of professional touring beast fighters (*venatores*); the text records their request for payment; Diana/Nemesis, goddess of hunting and good fortune, and a favourite of *venatores*, holds a large ear of wheat, a good luck symbol

SPITTARA

VICTOR

BVLLARIVS

CRISPINVS

Lead curse tablets have been found in many parts of the Roman empire – and some in amphitheatres, inscribed with the names of combatants and invoking deities to bring them evil fortune. The amphitheatres at Carthage and Trier had underground mortuary chambers containing many of these magic curses when excavated.

This is the first written evidence, however, of the cult of Diana from London. Diana was the goddess of the moon and sudden death, and had a particular association with amphitheatres and beast-fighting in her role as the 'divine huntress'. In or near amphitheatres Diana was also frequently venerated as Nemesis, the goddess of fortune and state justice. Together they appear on inscriptions at amphitheatres more than any other deity – not by or for those who fought in them so much as those who organised, sponsored or visited the shows.

Altars to Diana in amphitheatres are known from places as diverse as Zurich, Aquincum and Bonn. In Britain a plaque to Nemesis was found at the Caerleon amphitheatre – also concerning itself with stolen clothing – and there is also the Nemesis altar at Chester. The 4th-century AD mosaic at the Bignor villa, Sussex, has panels showing cupid-gladiators, whilst the central panel contains Diana. The same combination of seasonal motifs, gladiators and Diana has been noted in North African mosaics as well.

Specific chambers (shrines) dedicated to Nemesis/Diana have been identified within amphitheatres across Europe and Africa. It seems very likely that there was a shrine to Diana at the London amphitheatre – used mainly by people in the audience, as well as town magistrates, priests, officials and so on, those known as dedicants from other Diana/Nemesis shrines.

Apart from the link with animal fighting, Diana/Nemesis had a distinct role as a kind of symbol of the power of the Roman state – the goddess of justice. It is likely that displays of expensive professional gladiators were fairly rare in Britain: most shows were probably concerned with the execution of criminals, often through wild beasts. The presence of Diana/Nemesis presiding over such shows is entirely to be expected.

Image of Diana on a piece of imported samian pottery from the London amphitheatre

THE PINES OF ROME

Pine cones provide a heady perfume when burnt and were used extensively by the Romans for incense in rituals. *Pinus pinea* has been found at many sites in Britannia and Londinium. It has always been assumed that both cones and nuts were imported, but recent excavations suggest that the tree may have been deliberately introduced to this country. At the Guildhall pine cones were found in a ditch fill and fragile pine tree branches were found on the edge of the ditch, strongly suggesting that they could not have travelled far. The ditch, and thus the probable location of the tree from which they came, was only *c* 20m from the eastern entrance to London's amphitheatre. Perhaps a living tree supplied the incense for rituals associated with the opening or closing of the amphitheatre games.

Stone pine cone (right) found in a 2nd-century AD ditch outside the east entrance to the amphitheatre, with a modern example (left)

THE FIRST LONDON AMPHITHEATRE
FROM AD 74 TO THE EARLY 2ND CENTURY AD

London's first, timber, amphitheatre was probably built sometime in AD 74 or 75, as suggested by tree-ring dating of timbers used in the eastern entrance to the arena. Although Roman London had existed for nearly three decades by this time, the site had seen little use beyond some scattered quarrying of gravel and construction of surface drains. The long axis of the London amphitheatre was orientated almost due east–west, an alignment that differed from that of the surrounding street grid and may be explained by the Roman preference for positioning an amphitheatre's *tribunalia*, the raised platform for the seating of dignitaries, at the north or south compass points of the arena. It also took advantage of the local topography – notable for an area of lower ground crossed by small tributaries of the Walbrook stream. Timber beams, posts and planks from the structure were found during the excavations. The timbers were very well preserved, and accurate dates for when the trees were chopped down have been provided by tree-ring dating. Very little pottery or coins earlier than this date were found in the excavations.

Although only the eastern end of the amphitheatre was found, it is possible to calculate that it was *c* 87m long and 74m across. The arena featured an internal palisade wall estimated to enclose a surface area measuring 52m east–west and 39m north–south. The seating area (known as the *cavea* in Latin) held about ten tiers of wooden benches, constructed of planks nailed to a timber framework and seating nearly 7000 spectators. Entranceways into the arena would have passed through or under the seating tiers at the eastern and western ends of the amphitheatre.

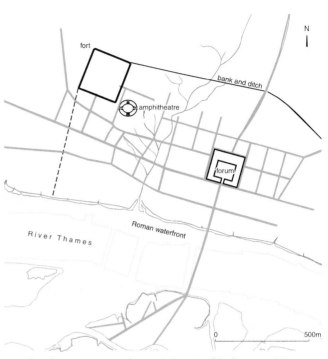

Map of Londinium in *c* AD 100, showing the location of the forum, amphitheatre and nearby fort

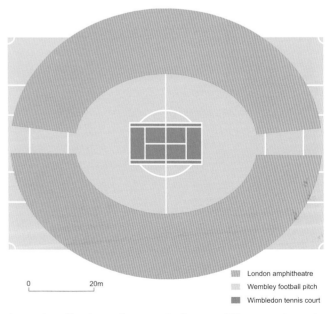

A comparison of London sporting arenas: the Roman amphitheatre superimposed on the Wembley Stadium football pitch and Wimbledon's centre court

London amphitheatre
Wembley football pitch
Wimbledon tennis court

Timber post and post pad located along the outer or eastern edge of the amphitheatre banking to the south of the eastern entranceway

The oval arena had been created by digging nearly 2m into the natural ground surface and then spreading out a layer of soft sand (the word *arena* means sand in Latin). Around the arena's perimeter was a timber wall, made from planks nailed to vertical, squared, timber posts, the bottoms of which were found in the excavation. Axe marks were still visible where the posts had been chopped down to make way for a rebuild of the amphitheatre.

Other, much larger, posts provided support for the tiers of seating around the arena, and flanked the entranceways. Though these posts had been removed during the Roman period, the deep pits dug to hold them were clearly identifiable and contained timber planks used as footings to support the upright posts.

A cross section through the bank and *cavea*, based on the size, spacing and depth of the posts and postholes to the south of the eastern entranceway, shows a possible reconstruction of the seating structure for the first timber amphitheatre. The structure is radially framed and supported with angled braces, techniques commonly used by Roman builders.

A row of deep pits for large timber posts flanking the eastern entrance into the arena of the original timber amphitheatre; the original timber bases on which the posts had been set can be seen at the bottom of the pits; this timber entranceway wall was later replaced by the stone wall to the left

Interpretative cross section through the timber amphitheatre bank and seating

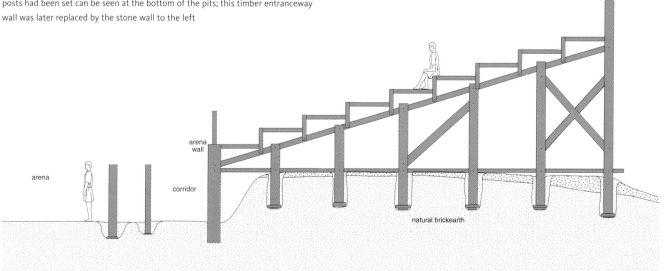

arena

arena
wall

corridor

natural brickearth

The Romans introduced Britain to an organised timber trade, techniques such as sawing, and the concept and practice of timber-frame building, involving the prefabrication of solid, closely jointed frames which could be assembled on site. All these innovations were prerequisites to building elaborate structures such as the timber amphitheatre. Specific Roman carpentry techniques included mortise-and-tenon and lap dovetail joints, complex scarf joints and the widespread use of iron nails for fixing. The Guildhall site has produced the best evidence for Roman sawyers' work in London. The techniques died out with the end of Roman rule and were not seen again in England for over 600 years.

Roman sawyers, *sectores materium*, at work

A timber block used to support one of the posts for the amphitheatre seating gantry had markings stamped into the surface of the wood, including the letters ICLV and MIBL, possibly associated with an official supplier of timber to public building projects

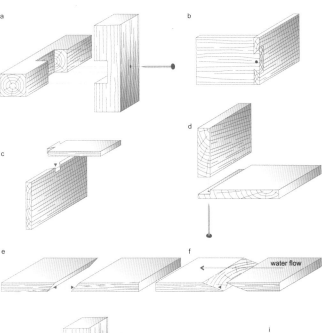

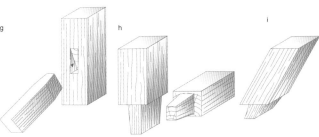

Roman woodworking joints found at the London amphitheatre: (a) halving secured with an iron spike; (b) single dovetail corner joint with one securing nail; (c) lap dovetail; (d) nailed rebate; (e) edge mitres; (f) through-splayed ends for unfastened drain planks; (g) sloping recess for infill staves in reused building timbers; (h) tapered stub tenons; (i) a chase stub tenon

Nick Bateman standing in the Roman amphitheatre at Fréjus in France, now used as a bullfighting ring; the arrangement of timber entrance gates, arena palisade wall and sliding doors for the bulls is strikingly similar to the evidence found at the London amphitheatre

The wooden gateway for the eastern entrance into the arena was a substantial structure, over 5m (c 16ft) wide. Some of the lowest gate timbers were found during the dig. They included two, very large wooden uprights which were jointed and nailed to a long horizontal beam at the arena's surface level. The tops of the uprights had been roughly hacked off when the amphitheatre was repaired and rebuilt. The surface of the horizontal 'threshold beam' was so well preserved that cuts and slots could be easily identified and must represent fittings for hinges and locks in a large two-leaf gate. Heavy wear in one small stretch of the gate suggests that a smaller 'wicket gate' was located within one side.

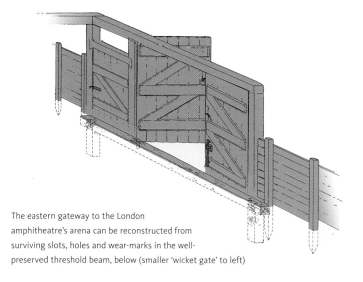

The eastern gateway to the London amphitheatre's arena can be reconstructed from surviving slots, holes and wear-marks in the well-preserved threshold beam, below (smaller 'wicket gate' to left)

TREE-RING DATING

Trees add a new growth-ring every year, the size of which varies according to the balance of rain and sun in that year. Because every year is different, every ring is different, but the pattern is the same for all trees of the same species from the same region. Thus, by working backwards from the present day, a given pattern (similar to a bar code or finger print) can be matched by an expert in the field, a dendrochronologist, with a particular period. If the wood is well preserved and the rings can be seen, a felling date can be worked out for most oak trees that grew in the London area over the last 4000 years.

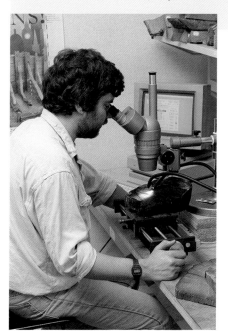

In the laboratory, dendrochronologist Ian Tyers examines the ring pattern of a tree-ring dating sample collected from the Guildhall

Two large timbers from the entranceway into the arena: the lower one is jointed with upright posts at each end; the gateway which existed over this threshold can be reconstructed (above); in the 2nd century AD a slightly narrower gateway was erected (the higher timber which retains the complex traces of the original structure over it)

A ROMAN BOTTLE BANK

Drains immediately to the east of the timber amphitheatre had decayed and collapsed in the early 2nd century AD, creating a muddy hole. This area was briefly used to dump unwanted debris and rubbish, including pottery and a huge amount of broken vessel glass and waste material from a glass workers' workshop. Over 58,000 fragments were recovered from the deposit, making it one of the most important glass assemblages from the north-western provinces of the Empire. Despite its importance, it is little more than a Roman 'bottle bank' mixed with the waste material from the daily production of glass vessels, together forming a dump of glass collected for recycling (cullet).

We cannot be certain why the Guildhall cullet dump was discarded, given the care that must have been taken to collect it. Perhaps more glass was collected for recycling than was actually needed or the glass workshop was closed or relocated. It is even possible that local glass working was evicted from the area during the rebuilding of the amphitheatre and development of the surrounding area in the early 2nd century AD.

Domestic waste including glass, pottery and organic rubbish was thrown into the boggy ground which developed to the east of the amphitheatre

Four pots, made locally at Highgate, found in dumps to the east of the amphitheatre

A selection of just some of the glass fragments recovered from the Guildhall cullet dump

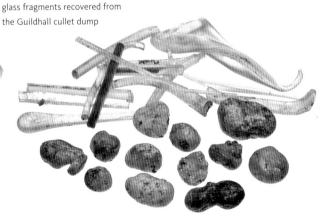

THE 'IMPROVED' AMPHITHEATRE
FROM *c* AD 120–30 TO THE MID 4TH CENTURY AD

The timber amphitheatre, or at least its eastern entrance, was modified or renovated sometime after AD 91, and then, sometime after the visit to Britain of the new emperor, Hadrian, in AD 122, London's amphitheatre was rebuilt and enlarged, partly in stone.

Archaeological evidence found across the City of London tells us that a fire destroyed a large area of the Roman settlement some time between AD 120 and AD 130. There was, however, no evidence of fire damage or redeposited fire debris at the site of the timber amphitheatre, even though it was rebuilt at about this time. Nevertheless it is tempting to suggest that the old, dilapidated amphitheatre was rebuilt as part of a general rejuvenation of the town after the fire.

Rebuilding of the main elements of the amphitheatre included the walls around the arena and flanking the entranceways. The new walls were constructed of Kentish ragstone and tile, replacing the earlier timber walls. Although a lot of the amphitheatre's masonry was dismantled in the late Roman period, some of the walls in the eastern entranceway survive to this day to a height of 1.5m (5ft) and are *c* 1m (3ft) thick. The walls were built of 3–5 successive courses of roughly-squared ragstone, followed by a double course of red tile used to ensure that the wall was level, with more ragstone courses then following above that. The stone walls were never higher than *c* 2.5m (8ft), being intended only to provide a base and facade for the arena perimeter, while the upper parts of the superstructure and seating continued to be built from timber. The height of the arena wall is similar to that of other British and Continental amphitheatres, and prevented wild animals or unruly gladiators from climbing into the audience.

A tile from the Guildhall site, stamped with the letters *PPBRLON*, which stands for the procurator of the province of Britannia at London; tiles with such stamps are commonly found near large public buildings and this may indicate some official involvement in the amphitheatre's construction

EMPEROR HADRIAN (AD 117–38)

Hadrian was thought of as one of the 'good' emperors; for instance, he changed the law so that slaves could no longer be sold to the arena by their masters for no particular reason. He was also a connoisseur of arms, had a thorough knowledge of warfare and knew how to use gladiatorial weapons himself. Dio tells us that he travelled extensively through the Empire, investigating and reforming, and 'he also constructed theatres and held games as he travelled about from city to city'. To celebrate his birthday 'he put into the arena a thousand wild beasts', while other writings tell us that: 'On his mother-in-law he bestowed especial honour by means of gladiatorial games'.

A bronze bust of Emperor Hadrian dredged from the Thames; Hadrian was known for his enthusiasm for restoring or enlarging public buildings throughout the Empire

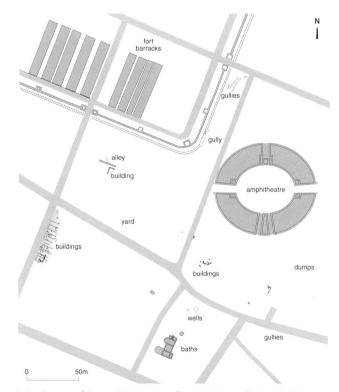

Redevelopment of the amphitheatre area after the Hadrianic fire included the rebuilding of the amphitheatre in stone and establishment of the nearby fort at Cripplegate

We have found enough of the rebuilt amphitheatre's walls to be able to make an estimate of its original size and shape. The arena wall enclosed an area *c* 57m east–west and 45m north–south, nearly identical to its timber predecessor, but the seating banks were wider, providing space for more rows of seating and indicating overall external dimensions of 98 x 87m. Comparison with other known amphitheatres and calculations for the number of square metres of seating area per person, suggested that the enlarged amphitheatre held between 7000 and 10,500 spectators (by comparison, the Royal Albert Hall has a capacity of just over 5000).

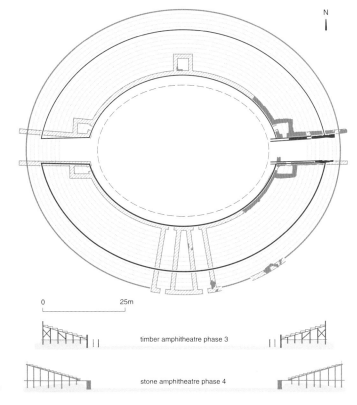

N

0   25m

timber amphitheatre phase 3

stone amphitheatre phase 4

Diagram showing the outline of the 1st-century AD timber amphitheatre and its 2nd-century replacement in stone

Kieron Heard drawing a detailed elevation of part of the entranceway wall

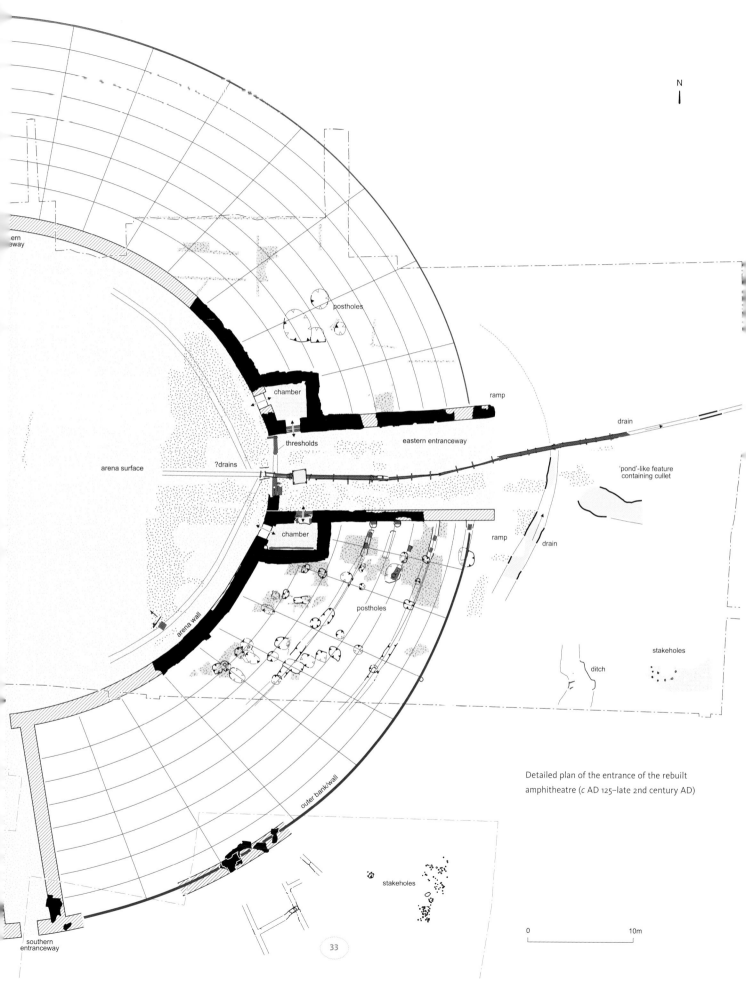

N

posthesoles

chamber

ramp

drain

eastern entranceway

thresholds

'pond'-like feature
containing cullet

arena surface

?drains

drain

ramp

chamber

stakeholes

posthesoles

ditch

arena wall

outer bank/wall

Detailed plan of the entrance of the rebuilt
amphitheatre (c AD 125–late 2nd century AD)

stakeholes

southern
entranceway

0   10m

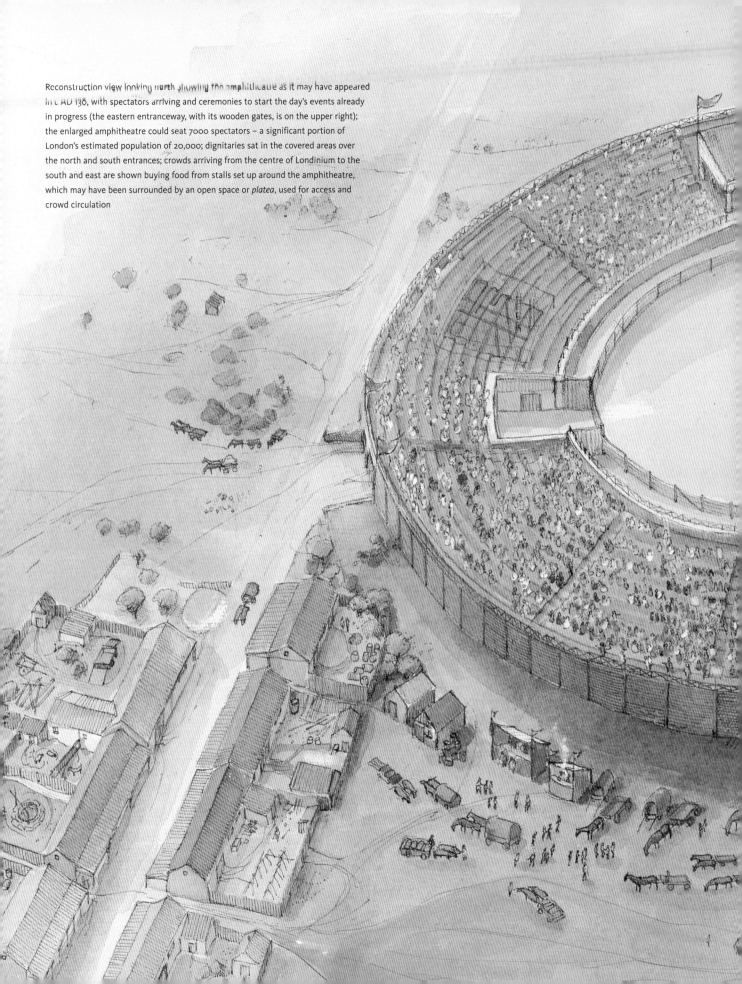

Reconstruction view looking north showing the amphitheatre as it may have appeared in c AD 130, with spectators arriving and ceremonies to start the day's events already in progress (the eastern entranceway, with its wooden gates, is on the upper right); the enlarged amphitheatre could seat 7000 spectators – a significant portion of London's estimated population of 20,000; dignitaries sat in the covered areas over the north and south entrances; crowds arriving from the centre of Londinium to the south and east are shown buying food from stalls set up around the amphitheatre, which may have been surrounded by an open space or *platea*, used for access and crowd circulation

The remodelled arena's eastern entranceway was *c* 7m (23ft) wide, and widened as it extended towards the eastern exit. Timber beams had been laid at different times in the masonry amphitheatre's life to form thresholds for the large double-leafed gates, which opened into the arena. Set into the upper surface of one of these timbers was a rectangular iron socket which may have acted as the pivot base for one of the gates.

Two large, rounded, capping stones were found in destruction debris at the foot of the arena wall and probably fell there during the final years of the amphitheatre's life. The remains of iron fittings were visible in the top of the curved stones, fixed in place with molten lead, providing evidence that a railing or grill ran along the top of the arena wall. Other slots in the stones may have held timbers used to support the protective netting that was sometimes raised to stop wild animals escaping.

A layer of thick pink mortar had been plastered on the inner face of the arena wall to give it a smooth finish and scatters of brightly painted plaster were found at the foot of the wall, perhaps having fallen from the wall as the amphitheatre fell into disrepair or disuse. Evidence from other British amphitheatres, such as Chichester, Chester and Caerleon, also suggests that the arena walls were plastered and painted. At Cirencester this seems to have been done as a trompe l'œil, painted to resemble marble. Some of the very large amphitheatres on the Continent even carried scenes of combat.

Fragments of imported marble inlays and mouldings were also found in the arena, including rare and costly Egyptian and Greek porphyry. Several thin pieces of Purbeck marble lay near the amphitheatre walls and may represent 'facings' from parts of the upper superstructure, perhaps the dignitaries' boxes (see illustration below).

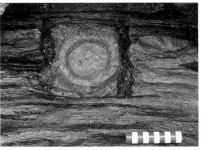

Later threshold timbers associated with the gateway at the eastern entrance to the arena (below Victorian brickwork); one timber contained an iron socket which had once housed the pivot for a gate (see detail below left)

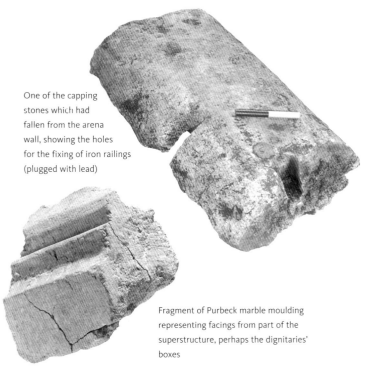

One of the capping stones which had fallen from the arena wall, showing the holes for the fixing of iron railings (plugged with lead)

Fragment of Purbeck marble moulding representing facings from part of the superstructure, perhaps the dignitaries' boxes

The earliest surface in the rebuilt arena was made of rammed gravel mixed with hard pink mortar and covered by a thinner layer of soft sand for a total thickness of *c* 10cm (4 inches). The combination of soft and hard layers may have been intentional and is seen repeated with successive resurfacings of the arena. The sand surface layer would have provided a soft bed to absorb the impact of falls, while the underlying harder layer would have provided some grip and prevented feet or hoofs from sinking. This surface construction was replicated in the mid 20th century when the makers of the film *Ben Hur* experimented with different surface types in order to stage the great chariot races round their reconstructed Circus Maximus. The elliptical arena of the London amphitheatre covered a large area and it seems that a full resurfacing was rarely carried out, perhaps due to the cost. Surface repairs were usually restricted to local patching where wear was particularly bad. Nevertheless, by the end of the amphitheatre's life the surface of the arena had been incrementally raised by over half a metre (2ft).

Chariot racing, as depicted in the film *Ben Hur*

A view across the sand surface of the arena; fragments of the arena wall can be seen curving from the bottom left to the top right of the photograph

As with most other British examples (with the exception of Chester and Caerleon), there was no evidence to prove that the London amphitheatre ever had an outer stone wall. This made it quite different in design to an amphitheatre such as the Colosseum in Rome. The walls flanking the London amphitheatre's eastern entranceway became progressively less high as they extended away from the arena, and the majority of deep postholes associated with the timber seating gantry were within 16m (52ft) of the arena wall, suggesting that the seating tiers did not extend all the way to the back of the entranceway and that the outer edge of the amphitheatre was built on a raised earth embankment. However, not all of the evidence is consistent with this interpretation, as footings recorded near the southern entranceway could be related to an external staircase built against an external masonry wall.

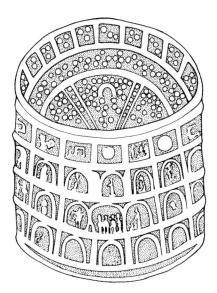

Representation of the Flavian amphitheatre (Colosseum), taken from a coin minted under Emperor Titus, son of Vespasian, in whose reign (AD 79–81) the Colosseum was formally opened; for the opening, Titus staged spectacular shows over 100 days, with thousands of gladiators and 9000 wild beasts slaughtered; women *venatores* were also exhibited

The Colosseum in Rome, the largest amphitheatre in the Roman world, could seat over 50,000 spectators

Alison Steele recording a stone-packed posthole along the outside of the London amphitheatre's timber seating; posts may have helped to revet a raised earth embankment beneath the seating area, taking the place of a stone external wall

One of the support posts for the seating gantry; the planks beneath the post made it firmer and slowed down rotting from rising damp

External staircases provided spectator access at several amphitheatres, including Pompeii, and recent excavations at the Chester amphitheatre have confirmed that external stairs were built against the outer wall there to provide access to the highest rear seats. It may be that the London amphitheatre's outer wall was a hybrid affair that included lengths of sloping embankment but with external masonry walls and even stairs near the entrances.

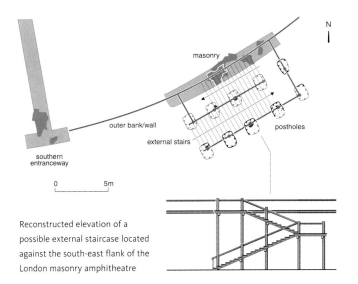

Reconstructed elevation of a possible external staircase located against the south-east flank of the London masonry amphitheatre

London's amphitheatre may have looked quite similar to this part-masonry, part-timber amphitheatre depicted on Trajan's column in Rome, erected in c AD 125 to celebrate the emperor's victory in the new province of Dacia (Romania)

East–west cross section through the London masonry amphitheatre's seating bank, showing the possible arrangement of support posts and bracing as well as the relation of the seating to the arena

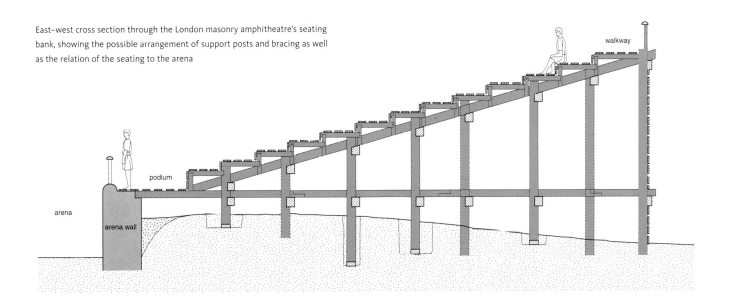

The amphitheatre's drains

Although drainage may not sound like an exciting topic, one of the most important and informative discoveries made during the Guildhall excavation was the amphitheatre's complex system of drains, which had survived in remarkable condition thanks to the wet soil conditions. The London amphitheatre's arena was set in a sunken area cut into the ground, meaning that it was a collecting point for surface rain-water and rising ground-water. To cope with this problem, the Roman architects devised a network of timber drains running under and around the arena and the eastern entrance.

The drains ranged in design from simple stone-lined gullies with plank covers, located around the perimeter of the arena, to sophisticated, fully carpentered, box drains that ran along the main east–west axis of the amphitheatre and carried water eastwards through the eastern entranceway and eventually to the Walbrook stream. Complex joints survived between the drain timbers and there was extensive evidence of marks associated with the adzes, saws and chisels used to hew them, giving us a privileged look inside a Roman carpenter's toolbox.

The water flowing through the drains under the amphitheatre also carried a lot of silt and rubbish that could clog and block the system. The Romans had very simple but effective solutions for this danger. The large plank-lined tank shown below lay along the course of the main drain, with water flowing into it from the left and out again to the right. Any sediment or other material settled at the bottom of the sump, which would have been emptied regularly – probably by a slave standing in the sump in much the same way as the archaeologist shown below.

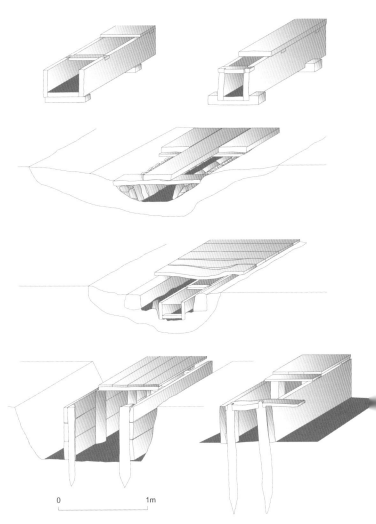

Reconstructions showing the different types of timber drains found in the amphitheatre

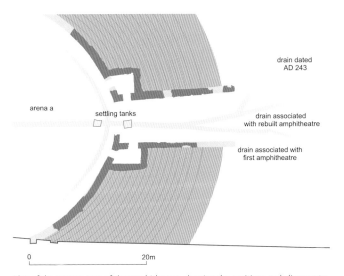

drain dated
AD 243

arena a

settling tanks

drain associated
with rebuilt amphitheatre

drain associated with
first amphitheatre

0   20m

Plan of the eastern part of the amphitheatre, showing the positions and alignments of the major phases of drains which carried water from the arena eastwards

The drains were rebuilt at various times throughout the lifetime of the amphitheatre. Sometimes repair was piecemeal, replacing a rotten timber here, a broken plank there, but at other times a more radical overhaul was necessary. This was particularly true in the early 2nd century AD when the area just outside the eastern entrance of the amphitheatre seems to have turned into a bog, perhaps due to more general problems with drainage in the Walbrook valley to the north-east, until new drains were installed. Timber drains were also rebuilt at higher levels as the ground surface rose in the arena. The latest repair of a drain for which we have specific tree-ring dating evidence took place in AD 243 or shortly afterwards. Other dating evidence suggests that the drains and the arena surface were maintained until the very end of the 3rd century AD.

One of the later timber drains along the perimeter of the arena can be seen on the left, adjacent to one of the eastern entranceway's side chambers

Three of the many Roman coins found in the amphitheatre drains

Detail of oak planks, expertly fitted together with dovetail corner joints and one securing nail, forming part of a water tank linked with the amphitheatre drains

Photographs showing the central east–west aligned timber drain in the arena, with its original plank covering in place (left) and partially removed (right); the drains would originally have been covered by the sand surface of the arena

The amphitheatre's southern entrance

The latest excavation on the amphitheatre site was carried out in autumn 1999. Although only a small trench was dug, this excavation demonstrated conclusively that there was a southern entrance into the amphitheatre. The layout and alignment of the fragmentary stone walls suggest that there were probably two entrance passages leading into the arena from the south, perhaps joining together in a single chamber just behind the arena wall. Similar arrangements are known from several other amphitheatres in Britain and on the Continent. It is quite likely that it was through these passages, running beneath the seating area, that some of the audience also made their way to their seats. These passages might also have connected to stairs leading up to the *tribunalia*, the box for the presiding dignitaries, which usually lay along one or both of an amphitheatre's short axes, in this case the north–south one.

Ian Blair examining a human skeleton found just behind the small fragment of wall in the southern entranceway to the arena

The compacted gravel surface of the ramped eastern entranceway leading to the arena

Animal fighting at the amphitheatre

Two small side chambers, built of stone, lay to the sides of the amphitheatre's eastern entrance passage, adjacent to the arena. Each chamber had two doorways, one leading into the arena and the other to the entrance passage. One of the chambers was probably used by fighters or fight officials as a kind of restroom, perhaps also including a small shrine for last-minute prayers. This was certainly the case at the Chester amphitheatre, where a similar room was excavated in the 1960s. The room there contained an inscribed stone altar to the goddess Nemesis (fate or justice), and burning marks in front of the altar indicate the location of an incense brazier.

A total of 324 mould-decorated samian vessels – high-quality imported tableware – recovered from the Guildhall excavations included 17 that show gladiators and other scenes from the arena. The pots may have been sold as souvenirs of the shows or used in the provision of refreshments for spectators, but many are large and expensive vessels which may have been used for offerings at the fighters' shrines, or perhaps even at the pre-games banquets known to have been given to the combatants by the donor of the games and to which the public may have been admitted. The most interesting of the London amphitheatre bowls was found outside the eastern entranceway and depicts a bullfighting scene, which is particularly intriguing given the discovery of a bull's skull in a nearby drain.

Stone altar found in a chamber at the Chester amphitheatre; the Latin inscription reads 'To the goddess Nemesis, Sextius Marcianus, the centurion, [set this up] after a vision'; Nemesis (fate) was often equated with Diana, the goddess of hunting, and small chambers dedicated to her service have been found at many amphitheatres across the Roman Empire

The 'bullfighting' bowl from the London amphitheatre showing a *venator* confronting a bull, with the corpses of three *damnati* slain by the bull, below; to the right is a satyr playing a double pipe, with Bacchus and a leopard beyond

Gladiators on decorated samian sherds from the London amphitheatre

There is no evidence from amphitheatres in Britain for exotic wild beasts, which were slaughtered in large numbers at the Colosseum. British arenas probably witnessed the baiting of bulls, bears or boars rather than the use of lions, leopards or elephants – given the difficulty and expense of obtaining exotic creatures – but lions and leopards are shown on pots from the London amphitheatre.

Helen Jones uncovering the skull of a bull dropped or placed in the base of the London amphitheatre arena's perimeter drain

Scene showing a leopard and lion with warrior, dwarf or pigmy fighter on a samian bowl found at the London amphitheatre (left) and another sherd with a *venator* and leopard (right)

Detail from a mosaic showing a *venator* killing a leopard (Galleria Borghese, Rome)

SER PENIVS

Three of the London amphitheatre chambers' doorframes were built of wood, and the horizontal threshold timbers were found during excavation, but one doorway leading from the southern chamber into the arena used two massive stone blocks as a threshold. These had clearly been reused from an earlier building, but deep narrow slots cut into their upper surfaces were clearly meant to function with an entrance into the arena. Pairs of these slots, only 40mm (1 1/2 inches) apart, were set on either side of the door opening. There are no obvious parallels for these in London but it seems likely that they represent part of a frame for operating a sliding, raisable, timber trapdoor. Roman amphitheatres had complex arrangements for the release of wild beasts into the arena: the most famous example being the Colosseum, where a labyrinth of underground cells, passage ways, movable ramps and lifts, all operated by slaves using ropes and pulleys, allowed the safe movement of hundreds of lions, tigers, elephants and other animals into the arena. Evidence for sliding vertical trapdoors has been found at other amphitheatres, for example Lepcis Magna in North Africa.

A small Roman oil lamp (left) decorated with the image of a boar, and (right) a boar on a piece of imported samian; boars may have been baited in the London arena from which these pieces came

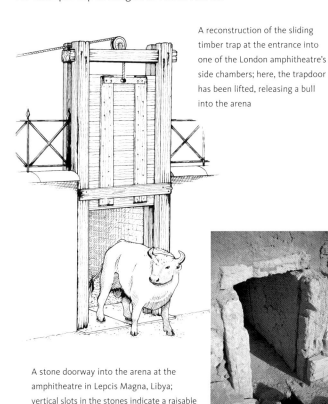

A reconstruction of the sliding timber trap at the entrance into one of the London amphitheatre's side chambers; here, the trapdoor has been lifted, releasing a bull into the arena

A stone doorway into the arena at the amphitheatre in Lepcis Magna, Libya; vertical slots in the stones indicate a raisable trapdoor, just as proposed at London

Valerie Griggs cleaning the masonry doorway leading into a side chamber for wild animals, to the left, with the arena to the right; the paired mortise slots cut into the threshold stones are interpreted as being for support beams associated with a sliding trapdoor

Who went to the London amphitheatre?

One of the most exciting aspects of the London amphitheatre's drains was the quantity of finds discovered in them, and the insight that these give us into the people who visited the arena or were somehow associated with its use. Archaeological work at sites across the city has helped us to identify the names of several hundred Roman Londoners, known from sources as varied as official inscriptions and graffiti on objects. Many of these must have visited the amphitheatre. At the highest level, visitors may have included the province's governors, men such as Petillius Cerialis, a personal friend of Emperor Vespasian. Others may have included soldiers seconded to London, such as the centurion Vivius Marcianus of the Second Legion, businessmen such as Rufus, son of Callisunus, whose name was found on a wooden writing tablet in the nearby Walbrook valley, a man called Turpillus who seems to have liked his drink (his name was engraved on a wine jar) and perhaps even the more fortunate slaves such as Anacletus, whose work was connected with running the emperor worship cult and whose tombstone has been found in London. The number of hairpins and other items indicating the presence of women suggests they made up a significant proportion of the audience at times.

Gold necklace clasp with chain and pearl, and an enamelled copper-alloy brooch; both found in the drains beneath the amphitheatre arena and possibly lost by a rich woman in the audience; contemporary writings contain many references to the attraction of wealthy women to well-built and successful gladiators; the eruption of Vesuvius in AD 79 entombed the city of Pompeii, and the body of a richly dressed woman was found where she died, apparently trying to flee from the gladiators' barracks

Stamped leather insole from a sandal found near the eastern entranceway to the amphitheatre

This graffiti from a tomb outside the Nucerian gate at Pompeii shows an encounter between the most famous of the *Neroniani* (*Princeps Neronianus*) and his defeated rival Creunus, with a tally of their fights and victories recorded beside them; the figures to the left may be spectators, with the buglers in the amphitheatre to the right; just as with football today, graffiti about individual gladiators and shows were widespread, and many referred to the alleged sexual attributes of the combatants

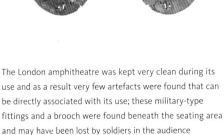

The London amphitheatre was kept very clean during its use and as a result very few artefacts were found that can be directly associated with its use; these military-type fittings and a brooch were found beneath the seating area and may have been lost by soldiers in the audience

Carved bone hairpins from the amphitheatre drains; such pins are often found on Roman sites and would have been used in the elaborate hairstyles that were fashionable among Roman women

A painting (1872) by the French artist Jean-Leon Gerome called *Pollice verso* (thumbs down): a gladiator has won his fight and awaits the signal to finish off his opponent; the right to spare a gladiator (*missio*) belonged to the person presenting the show (*editor*), though he was often influenced by the reaction of the crowd – here the vestal virgins in the front row express their opinion (a fight announced as *sine missione* meant a fight with no possible quarter)

Renovation and continued use of the amphitheatre

The enlarged masonry amphitheatre was the subject of repeated episodes of repair and renovation in the later 2nd and 3rd centuries AD. Most of the changes, at least those that survived to be recorded archaeologically, involved work on the entrances, the laying of new arena surfaces and frequent changes to the system of timber drains (see above). The arena wall was demolished and replaced by a narrower stone wall some time after AD 270, though it is not clear why this should have been done. At about this time the seating superstructure may also have been dismantled and removed before wholesale reconstruction. Such extensive work may have been necessary if the amphitheatre had fallen into serious disrepair. In any case it indicates a continuing need for a working amphitheatre in Roman London into the first years of the 4th century AD.

The narrower rebuild of the amphitheatre's arena wall to the south of the eastern entranceway, set on top of the partially robbed 2nd-century AD wall

Gladiatorial re-enactment on the site of the amphitheatre

A fragment of pottery from London showing a heavily armed gladiator

Opposite: aerial view across the eastern part of the amphitheatre at the end of the 1992–3 excavation; the massive steel structures were used to brace the sides of the dig as the excavation proceeded downwards; the curving wall of the arena can be seen beneath the steelwork, with the two small side chambers flanking the eastern entranceway to the left

AMPHITHEATRES IN BRITAIN

Apart from London, amphitheatre-like buildings have been identified at a number of places in Britain. All were largely earth-built structures, meaning that the arena was cut into the ground and the seating bank correspondingly raised. They were comparatively simple structures, far removed from the architectural extravagance of the Colosseum and similar monumental amphitheatres on the Continent. Only those British amphitheatres located at Caerleon and Chester, by the great legionary fortresses, and at the deserted town of Silchester, have been excavated to any great extent. On the other hand, several buildings which are often described as 'theatres', such as at St Albans, were probably hybrid structures with at least some amphitheatre functions. Frequently this type of building is found not in a town but linked with what might be called 'rural retreats' – pilgrimage centres with baths, temples and buildings for public shows. Examples have been found at Caistor (Norfolk), Frilford (Oxfordshire) and Gosbecks (Essex), and they were very common in Gaul (France).

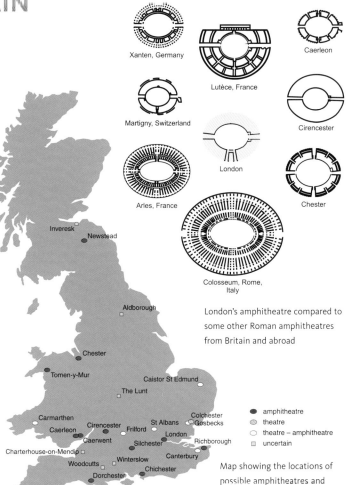

London's amphitheatre compared to some other Roman amphitheatres from Britain and abroad

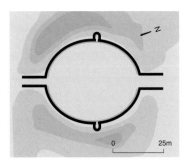

A plan of the amphitheatre at Silchester shows a masonry wall surrounding the arena and entranceways, with steep earth banks for the timber seating behind it

Map showing the locations of possible amphitheatres and associated 'structures of spectacle' in Roman Britain

- ● amphitheatre
- ◉ theatre
- ○ theatre – amphitheatre
- ▫ uncertain

THE BRITISH CONTRIBUTION

Dio writes that, following his conquest of Britain, the general Plautius was 'praised by Claudius but also received an ovation. In the gladiatorial combats many persons took part, not only of the foreign freedmen but also the British captives.' Martial, celebrating the opening of the Colosseum in AD 80, describes a criminal killed by an imported Caledonian (Scottish) bear. Indeed, a fragment of bone from a bear was found at the London amphitheatre and a bear skull has been recovered from a nearby site in the Walbrook valley. It is possible that dogfighting also took place in the London arena. Elsewhere, late Roman writings describe a show given by Emperor Gordian in the 3rd century AD in which stags from Britain were hunted.

The amphitheatre at Caerleon in Wales was closely linked to the nearby legionary fortress and was a substantial stone-built structure; the walls, seating banks and entranceways can all be seen here; the amphitheatre was in use from the 1st century until the end of the 3rd century AD

There is very little hard evidence for what actually went on in British amphitheatre arenas. Bones found at both London and Caerleon suggest that indigenous wild animals – boars, bears and wolves – were used, perhaps fighting each other, perhaps fighting *venatores*. There is some evidence for actual gladiators in the province: a gladiator's helmet found in Hawkedon, Suffolk, is very similar to types known from Pompeii, and what may be the trident of a *retiarius* was found in London. Archaeological evidence from St Albans might indicate that amphitheatres were used as places of public execution: a single deep post pit in the centre of the arena there has been interpreted as the stake to which criminals were tied. Though there were significant differences in scale, there is every reason to suspect that British amphitheatres were put to similar uses as those on the Continent. The grim likelihood is that, over a period of more than two centuries, thousands of animals and many men were slaughtered in London's arena.

Part of a mosaic found in the Roman villa at Bignor, West Sussex, shows gladiators humorously portrayed as winged *erotes* (cupids); although intentionally comic, the equipment is accurate

GLADIATORIAL IMAGES IN BRITAIN

There are very few British images of either gladiator or beast fighting in any form of visual decoration. One of the best known is the mosaic in the villa at Bignor, Sussex, which shows gladiators humorously portrayed as cupids. At Brading, on the Isle of Wight, there is a 4th-century AD mosaic showing gladiators fighting. At Eccles in Kent a 1st-century AD mosaic also shows fighting gladiators. A mosaic in the 4th-century AD villa in Rudstone, Yorkshire, shows a battle between wild animals and men. A 2nd-century AD frieze found at Chester, not far from the amphitheatre, depicts the victory of a *retiarius* over another gladiator. A 1st-century AD wall painting from a house in Colchester shows a defeated gladiator, while graffiti found in Leicester suggests that Lucius the gladiator loved Verecunda Ludia.

A 1st-century AD copper-alloy helmet found near Hawkedon in Suffolk; the helmet had been 'tinned' to appear bright silver, and is more than twice the weight of a legionary helmet; it is very similar to known gladiatorial helmets from Pompeii and was probably made in Italy

This trident head, found in London, may have belonged to a *retiarius* or net-fighter

A panel from a masonry frieze, found near the Chester amphitheatre, was probably from the tomb of a local *munerarius* (promoter) and shows a *retiarius* defeating another gladiator (broken off)

Part of a wall painting from a Roman house in Colchester; a defeated gladiator, who has put down his shield, holds his finger up in the standard gesture used in an appeal for mercy

THE END: LONDON'S AMPHITHEATRE ABANDONED

The London amphitheatre was abandoned sometime in the 4th century AD. A layer of grey silt, found covering the latest arena surface, contained pottery dated to c AD 300–400 as well as hundreds of shells of a particular type of water-loving snail. Together, this evidence suggests that the arena fell out of use and became waterlogged. The final use of the amphitheatre is not as clearly represented in the archaeological record as the robbing and dismantling of the abandoned structure, with activity associated with the demolition of the amphitheatre superstructure dated to the second half of the 4th century AD and probably to after c AD 364–5. Systematic removal of stonework and timbers for reuse elsewhere may have continued sporadically until the end of the 4th century AD.

Other activities post-dating the disuse of the amphitheatre included the disposal of three human burials, cut into the disused seating banks after c AD 365, as well as rubbish dumping and pit digging. It is impossible to say whether the use of the site as a dumping ground was organised or opportunistic, though it is possible that the derelict amphitheatre was used as a municipal dump for a time.

The three burials, all aged 17–25 years at time of death, are intriguing. Amphitheatre sites may have possessed a significance for Christians because of the connection with martyrdom, and if the individuals buried at the Guildhall were Christian then the choice of location might have had religious connotations, although the north–south alignment of two of them suggests that they were not. Other possible explanations for the presence of these late Roman burials are a decline in regulation leading to some unsanctioned use of abandoned areas within the city walls, or the disposal of murder victims or executed prisoners outside recognised cemeteries.

Horse, sheep and pig bones tossed into the latest backfill of the latest timber drain in the amphitheatre may indicate that the area became a dumping ground

David Lakin excavating collapsed red wall plaster from the remains of a building located near the east entrance of the amphitheatre

Most of the amphitheatre's masonry walls were robbed, that is, intentionally dug out to salvage and reuse the building material, though some parts simply collapsed or eroded. The robbing did not seem to be part of a single, organised plan, though we might imagine that the timber superstructure was probably removed first and taken away before it rotted. A lot of robbing of masonry buildings across Roman London took place in the late 4th century AD, probably to repair and reconstruct the city defensive walls at a time when there was a collapse of Roman power and authority throughout the Empire.

After abandonment and robbing the amphitheatre slowly became covered by a thick blanket of grey earth, commonly known as 'dark earth', associated with soil formation processes. The site of the amphitheatre lay fallow, surviving only as an oval depression in the ground.

A blanket of 'dark earth', over 1m (3ft) thick, sealed the abandoned remains of the Roman amphitheatre; such deposits, frequently found at City of London archaeological sites, give little clue as to what went on during the next 500 years, before the city was reoccupied in the 9th century AD

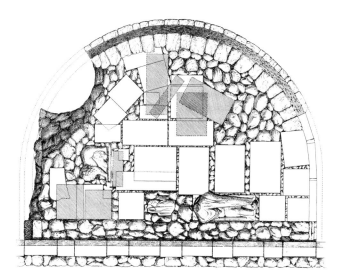

A drawing showing Roman statuary and other architectural fragments reused as rubble in the core of a late 4th-century AD tower added to the city's defences

Bezel of a late Roman silver finger ring engraved with a lion looking over its shoulder; from the 'dark earth' deposit at the amphitheatre

THE END OF ROMAN BRITAIN

By the 4th century AD Londinium was in decline: large parts of the walled area had been cleared of buildings and covered by a gradual accumulation of 'dark earth'. What remained of the Roman army in Britain reportedly withdrew in AD 407, and from AD 410 onwards there was no Roman governor in Britain. London became redundant as an imperial administrative and military centre: the archaeological evidence strongly suggests that Roman urban occupation in London ceased altogether at the time of the Roman withdrawal or soon after.

The secession from Rome meant the rapid disappearance of the Romanised economy. With neither pottery nor coins in circulation, the British population becomes difficult to detect and it seems that those who formerly inhabited the towns of Roman Britain withdrew to the countryside. The late 4th and early 5th centuries AD were, therefore, a period of increasing political and social instability, and pagan Germanic immigrants, the Anglo-Saxons, gained political control of a substantial part of south-eastern Britain by the mid 5th century AD.

Despite painstaking excavations over a large area, archaeological work at the Guildhall found no convincing evidence for activity in and around the old amphitheatre in the centuries following Rome's abandonment of Britain. Reoccupation of this part of London apparently did not begin for over 500 years, the first significant activity being the establishment of small buildings along a lane around the beginning of the 11th century.

In the absence of much archaeological evidence from the site, we must turn to historical documents for information. We know that Britain reconnected with European written history in AD 597, when Augustine arrived on a mission to convert the heathen English. In AD 604 Mellitus was appointed as the first new bishop of London, though he was driven from the area after a decade and the town did not properly become Christian until AD 675. Coins were being minted again in London by AD 640, the first since the collapse of Roman rule, but where was this 'London'?

THE WORK OF GIANTS

The Anglo-Saxons, ancestors of the English, were in awe of Roman remains. They feared them and tried to avoid them. An Old English poem relates how 'cities are visible from afar, the cunning work of giants'. The English were much given to pondering the ravages of time: another poem notes how 'the old works of the giants stood desolate'. A poem called 'The ruin' describes an entire town: 'wondrous is this wall-stone; broken by fate, the castles have decayed, the work of giants is crumbling'.

Writing in the early 12th century, Geoffrey of Monmouth noted that 'in earlier times Britain was graced with 28 cities. Some of these, in the depopulated areas, are now mouldering away, with their walls broken'. Even as late as the 14th century a monk could write of one northern town: 'it seemeth that it hath been founded by the painful labour of Romans or giants'.

Artist's impression of the ruins of Roman London, which quickly became overgrown after abandonment in the early 5th century AD

The deserted city defined by the Roman defensive walls is thought to have been reinstated as a seat of authority in the 7th century AD, comprising the cathedral church of St Paul and perhaps a royal residence. What is more certain is that a small settlement was established to the west of the city walls, along the curving north bank of the river known as the Strand. By the late 7th century AD this area had developed into the major trading port of Lundenwic, known from the writings of the 8th-century historian Bede, who described it as a 'trading centre for many nations who visit it by land and sea'. Archaeological excavations around St Martin-in-the Fields and Covent Garden suggest that Lundenwic thrived until the 9th century AD, when increasingly persistent Viking attacks forced the population to scatter. The more defensible site of the old Roman city was reoccupied in the late 9th century AD.

The remains of the amphitheatre were progressively buried beneath a layer of 'dark earth' during this time. This wind-blown and water-lain soil contained few artefacts and blanketed the arena and its surrounding seating banks, leaving no clue to the area's former use beyond a boggy hollow.

The development of streets and buildings around the site of the former amphitheatre from the 11th century onwards

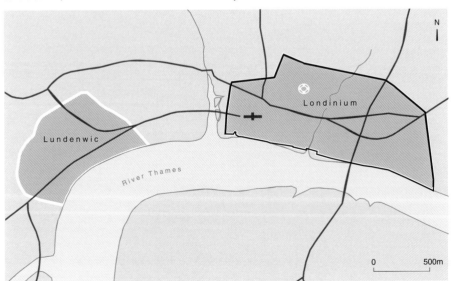

Map showing the location of Saxon Lundenwic along the Strand, in modern-day Covent Garden, to the west of the deserted walled Roman city

The yellow sandy surfaces of the arena can be seen here, sealed by half a metre (2ft) of 'dark earth' associated with Roman London's abandonment

Then, as the reoccupied walled city expanded northwards from the Thames, people finally returned to live here. A roughly cobbled north–south path was established across the area, with simple timber and wattle buildings constructed along its sides used as houses, workshops and byres for animals. Fences were built, ditches dug and pits excavated for the disposal of rubbish. The focus of this occupation seems to have been the slightly lower ground of the former arena. A burial ground was established immediately to the south-west and was probably associated with a church or chapel.

The path became a town lane in the 12th century and was extended northwards to the new Guildhall, built over the site of the amphitheatre's northern seating bank. The Guildhall and its precinct, the centre of government of the City of London, is now thought to date from the 1120s. In the 13th century the area of the lane was widened into an open space in front of the Guildhall, eventually becoming Guildhall Yard.

A detailed description of the early medieval archaeology and history of the amphitheatre site, and the later development of the Guildhall and its precinct, can be found in the main archaeological publication of the findings (*Further reading*, below).

Archaeologists found ephemeral evidence of wattle fences and timber buildings as well as a cobbled lane and cemetery – associated with 11th-century settlement in the area of the former amphitheatre arena

Artist's reconstruction view of 11th-century timber and wattle buildings huddled along the sides of a lane crossing the amphitheatre area; the church of St Lawrence lies to the south, the first Guildhall was built to the north in the early 12th century

The new Guildhall Art Gallery building includes a large part of the masonry amphitheatre, preserved as a permanent exhibition in the first basement level of the gallery. The shape of the amphitheatre's arena wall has also been marked out on the resurfaced Guildhall Yard, a line of slate slabs curving across the otherwise geometric pattern of paving stones, providing a permanent reminder of its underlying heritage.

The redesign of the Guildhall Art Gallery to allow preservation of London's Roman amphitheatre helped to realise two major goals. The most obvious was the actual conservation of the surviving physical remains of the amphitheatre which had been uncovered during the excavation, allowing the public display of an important archaeological discovery. Equally important was the recognition that the excavated sites represent just part of the archaeological remains lying beneath the Guildhall precinct, with a need for its careful management and significant potential for further discoveries.

The preservation of the amphitheatre's structural remains required complex design and engineering works, which began in 1994 and progressed alongside the archaeological excavations and overall construction programme until the opening of the new art gallery building in 1999. Work on the display and presentation of the preserved remains followed, and the display was opened to the public in 2002, though the conservation of the amphitheatre's timber drains continued and they were finally returned to the amphitheatre in 2006.

The requirement to preserve a Roman building within a modern one was an unusual and challenging job for the project's engineers. The design of foundation piles and floors in the new building had to be changed. In order to preserve the amphitheatre remains exactly where they had been found, their stone walls had to be suspended on a floor level above two deeper art gallery basements, an enormously elaborate undertaking in engineering terms. The Roman walls and foundations, together with an underlying wedge of natural gravel, had to be stabilised and then underpinned. The overall weight of the preserved and suspended block of material was enormous.

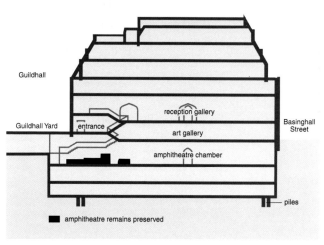

A simplified cross section through the new Guildhall Art Gallery, showing the level at which the amphitheatre walls were found and are now displayed

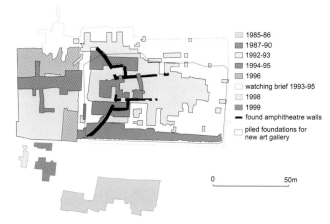

The Guildhall Yard excavations took place over many years as construction work progressed, illustrated by this quilt-work of excavation areas; the area of the Guildhall Art Gallery itself – shown here by a red line – contains a triple basement and required the complete removal of archaeological remains except for the preserved amphitheatre walls; excavation of a single basement elsewhere has allowed some archaeological strata to be preserved

Opposite: view east to the new Guildhall Art Gallery, with the line of the Roman amphitheatre's arena wall picked out in slates set into the surface of Guildhall Yard

Boxing and protecting the amphitheatre remains during construction work

The first step in the preservation process was to protect the amphitheatre walls during construction work. The stonework was encased in polythene and plywood boxing was then built around the walls and filled with expanding spray foam to dampen any vibration or movement. A crash deck was then built above the amphitheatre remains so that heavy machinery and other construction activity was separated from the archaeological levels.

Before the Roman walls could be underpinned it was necessary to remove any trapped groundwater from the area and extract any water within the walls themselves. The amphitheatre walls and foundations might crack if allowed to dry too quickly and the rate of drying was carefully monitored, using sensors placed at 28 locations.

The actual underpinning of the Roman foundations was both unconventional and ingenious. Perforated horizontal tubes were inserted into the natural gravel below the Roman masonry and injected with an epoxy grout. This passed through the perforations to fill any voids beneath the base level of the foundations. Completion of underpinning created a concrete base nearly 1m (3ft) thick which was then bonded into the main floor slab for the first basement level. Two further art gallery basement levels beneath the amphitheatre remains were then safely excavated by heavy machinery. The condition of the Roman foundations and walls was monitored throughout the construction and conservation process, and no damage was observed.

The amphitheatre also included important timber structures and these presented their own challenges. Most of the timbers had survived in excellent condition for nearly 2000 years due to the localised waterlogging within the sunken arena area, but once excavated or exposed to air they would quickly begin to deteriorate. Roman timbers were retained for study and dating and a large proportion of these were stored wet for possible display. The final selection for display *in situ* included a 6m-long (20ft) section of the main east–west drain found beneath the eastern entranceway to the arena, a 3m-long (10ft) section of the same drain beneath the arena itself, and an associated silt trap, and two thresholds for gateways leading to the side chambers.

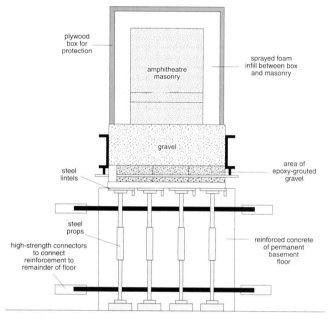

Diagram showing method used to underpin the Roman foundations

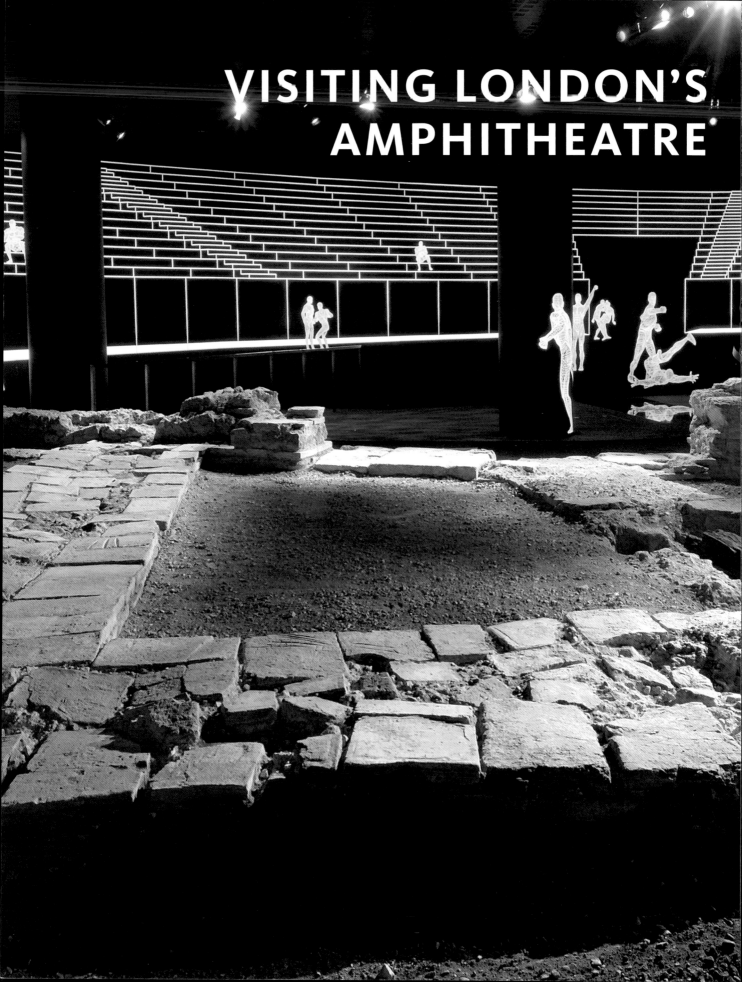

VISITING LONDON'S AMPHITHEATRE

Rather than create a conventional museum it was decided that the display of the amphitheatre, cocooned in the Guildhall Art Gallery basement, should emphasise the architecture of the Roman structure whilst recreating the drama of entering the arena.

The display is approached through the first basement level of the Guildhall Art Gallery. Visitors walk through the art exhibition rooms until they arrive at a series of introductory panels and display cases. These describe the amphitheatre and some of the activities which took place in it, with the arena glimpsed through a slit window. You then enter the darkened chamber containing the Roman remains through the original eastern entranceway of the amphitheatre. A carefully lit, perspex back panel recreates the perspective of the tiered seating and evokes the atmosphere and spatial sense of the amphitheatre. Luminous, perspex, 'wire-frame' human figures enhance the sense of perspective, whilst also suggesting the idea of digital reconstruction.

The display includes the amphitheatre's arena wall, the walls along the eastern entranceway and the two side chambers that were used to pen up animals or gladiators next to the arena. The preserved timber drain system running beneath the entranceway is visible beneath a glass surface set into the floor of the display. Of course, not all of the amphitheatre structure survived in antiquity or could be preserved, and the position of missing timber and stone structures is marked in metal strips set into the floor. Information panels are strategically positioned through the exhibition.

Artefacts on show in the display cases include the gold and pearl necklace clasp and an elaborately carved bone hairpin (above, pp 46–7), as well as coins, cooking utensils and drinking vessels, all of which illustrate the activity surrounding the amphitheatre in its heyday. The famous 'bullfighting' bowl (above, p43) and decorative brooches and buckles (these recovered from under the arena's seating areas and probably lost by spectators) are also featured.

PLACES TO VISIT

Guildhall Art Gallery and Roman London's amphitheatre
Guildhall Yard, London EC2V 5AE
tel: 020 7332 3700
http://www.guildhall-art-gallery.org.uk
for the impressively preserved remains of the eastern end of the amphitheatre in the basement below the art gallery; note that the line of the amphitheatre's curving arena wall is marked out in slate on the surface of Guildhall Yard, to the west of the art gallery

Museum of London: Roman London gallery
London Wall, London EC2Y 5HN
tel: 0870 444 3852 (national call rates in UK) +44 (0)20 7600 3699
http://www.museumoflondon.org.uk
for an extensive display of Roman London finds and interpretation of important themes

British Museum
Great Russell Street, London WC1B 3DG
tel: +44 (0)20 7323 8299
http://www.britishmuseum.org/explore/galleries/europe/room_49_roman_britain.aspx
for Roman finds from London and the Thames

Opposite: view of the amphitheatre display beneath the Guildhall Art Gallery, looking west across the southern side chamber of the eastern entranceway, with the arena in the background

FURTHER READING

J P V D Balsdon, 1969 *Life and leisure in ancient Rome*, London

Nick Bateman, 2009 What's the point of London's amphitheatre? A clue from Diana, in *Roman amphitheatres and spectacula: a 21st-century perspective: papers from an international conference held at Chester, 16–18 February, 2007* (ed Tony Wilmott), Oxford

Nick Bateman, Carrie Cowan and Robin Wroe-Brown, 2008 *London's Roman amphitheatre: excavations at the Guildhall*, MoLAS Monograph Series 35, London

David L Bomgardner, 2000 *The story of the Roman amphitheatre*, London and New York

David Bowsher, Tony Dyson, Nick Holder and Isca Howell, 2007 *The London Guildhall: an archaeological history of a neighbourhood from early medieval to modern times*, MoLAS Monograph Series 36, London

John Clark, Jon Cotton, Jenny Hall, Roz Sherris and Hedley Swain (eds), 2008 *Londinium and beyond: essays on Roman London and its hinterland for Harvey Sheldon*, CBA Research Report, York

Lindsey Davis, 1998 *Two for the lions*, London

Julian Hill and Peter Rowsome, 2011 *Roman London and the Walbrook stream crossing: excavations at 1 Poultry and vicinity*, MOLA Monograph Series 37, London

Elizabeth Howe and David Lakin, 2004 *Roman and medieval Cripplegate, City of London: archaeological excavations 1992–8*, MoLAS Monograph Series 21, London

Barri Jones and David Mattingly, 1990 *An atlas of Roman Britain*, Oxford

MOLA, 2011 *Londinium: a new map and guide to Roman London*, London

MoLAS, 2000 *The archaeology of Greater London: an assessment of archaeological evidence for human presence in the area now covered by Greater London*, London

Ordnance Survey, 2001 *Historical map and guide to Roman Britain*, 5 edn, Southampton

Dominic Perring, 1991 *Roman London: the archaeology of London*, London

Cathy Ross and John Clark, 2008 *London: an illustrated history*, London

Peter Rowsome, 2000 *Heart of the city: Roman, medieval and modern London revealed by archaeology at 1 Poultry*, London

Chris Thomas with Andy Chopping and Tracy Wellman (eds), 2003 *London's archaeological secrets: a world city revealed*, New Haven and London

Ben Weinreb, Christopher Hibbert, Julia Keay and John Keay, 2008 (rev edn) *The London encyclopaedia*, London

Katherine Welch, 2007 *The Roman amphitheatre: from its origins to the Colosseum*, New York

Thomas Wiedemann, 1992 *Emperors and gladiators*, London and New York

Tony Wilmott, 2008 *The Roman amphitheatre in Britain*, Stroud

Short articles on the archaeology of Roman London can also be found in:

The London Archaeologist (http://www.londonarchaeologist.org.uk),

the *Transactions of the London and Middlesex Archaeological Society* (http://www.lamas.org.uk)

and the *Journal of the Surrey Archaeological Society* (http://www.surreyarchaeology.org.uk).

KEY DATES

55–4 BC	Julius Caesar invades southern Britain but withdraws
up to AD 43	Rome enters into treaties and trade with kingdoms in southern Britain
AD 43	Claudius invades Britain and conquers the south-east
AD 47	Londinium founded, based on dated archaeological evidence
AD 50s	Roman roads, garrisons and towns established across the lowlands of Britain; Londinium grows rapidly
AD 60–1	Boudica rebels against Rome; Londinium destroyed
AD 60s	Londinium rebuilt
AD 74	London's amphitheatre constructed in timber
AD 70s/80s	Roman occupation expands to Wales and southern Scotland; Londinium grows as a commercial centre, with a public building programme including waterfronts, the first forum and public baths
AD 120–30	London's amphitheatre rebuilt in stone and on a larger scale
AD 122	Hadrian visits Britain in AD 122
AD 125	Londinium is largely destroyed by fire
AD 130–60	Roman London rebuilt but slowly declines as a commercial centre
AD 200	Defensive wall built to enclose Londinium's main settlement
AD 250–300	Londinium's defences strengthened with a riverside wall but the population falls and some public buildings are abandoned
AD 300–50	Edict of Milan grants toleration of Christianity in AD 313; Londinium suffers long-term decline
AD 350–400	Barbarians cross the Rhine; Britain attacked by Picts and Irish; Londinium adds defensive bastions to its walls but continues to shrink
AD 408–9	Roman government unable to defend Britain
AD 410	Visigoths sack Rome; Roman government ceases to control Britain
after AD 410	Londinium's remaining residents abandon the settlement as urban life becomes unsustainable